Poetry

Chicken, Shadow, Moon & More, 2000
Blizzard of One, 1998
Dark Harbor, 1993
Reasons for Moving, Darker, & The Sargentville Notebook, 1992
The Continuous Life, 1990
Selected Poems, 1980
The Late Hour, 1978
The Story of Our Lives, 1973
Darker, 1970
Reasons for Moving, 1968
Sleeping with One Eye Open, 1964

Prose

The Weather of Words, 2000
Mr. and Mrs. Baby, 1985
The Monument, 1978

Translations

Looking for Poetry, 2002
Travelling in the Family (poems by Carlos Drummond de Andrade)
    (with Thomas Colchie), 1986
The Owl's Insomnia (poems by Rafael Alberti), 1973

Art Books

Hopper, 2001
William Bailey, 1987
Art of the Real, 1983

For Children

Rembrandt Takes a Walk, 1986
The Night Book, 1985
The Planet of Lost Things, 1982

Anthologies

100 Great Poems of the Twentieth Century, 2005
The Golden Ecco Anthology, 1994
The Best American Poetry 1991 (with David Lehman)
Another Republic (with Charles Simic), 1976
New Poetry of Mexico (with Octavio Paz), 1970
The Contemporary American Poets, 1969

MAN AND CAMEL

Man and Camel

POEMS

MARK STRAND

ALFRED A. KNOPF   NEW YORK   2006

THIS IS A BORZOI BOOK
PUBLISHED BY ALFRED A. KNOPF

www.aaknopf.com

Knopf, Borzoi Books, and the colophon are
registered trademarks of Random House, Inc.

Library of Congress Cataloging-in-Publication Data
Strand, Mark, [date]
Man and camel : poems / by Mark Strand. — 1st ed.
p.   cm.
ISBN 0-307-26296-0
I. Title.
PS3569.T69M36 2006
811'.54—dc22   2006040986

Manufactured in the United States of America
Published September 7, 2006
Second Printing, November 2006

To Charles Simic
and Charles Wright

Contents

TWO

THREE

Acknowledgments

The author wishes to thank the editors of the following publications where these poems originally appeared, sometimes in slightly different form:

Brick: "Fire," "I Had Been a Polar Explorer"

Colorado Review: "Marsyas"

Final Edition: "The Webern Variations"

Meridian: "Elevator"

The New York Review of Books: "2002," "Error," "People Walking Through the Night"

The New Yorker: "2032," "Afterwords," "Black Sea," "The King," "Man and Camel," "Mirror," "Moon," "My Name," "The Rose," "Storm," "Two Horses"

Ploughshares: "Conversation"

Slate: "Mother and Son"

TriQuarterly: "Cake"

Verse: "Poem After the Seven Last Words"

ONE

The King

I went to the middle of the room and called out,
"I know you're here," then noticed him in the corner,
looking tiny in his jeweled crown and his cape
with ermine trim. "I have lost my desire to rule,"
he said. "My kingdom is empty except for you,
and all you do is ask for me." "But Your Majesty—"
"Don't 'Your Majesty' me," he said, and tilted his head
to one side and closed his eyes. "There," he whispered,
"that's more like it," and he entered his dream
like a mouse vanishing into its hole.

I Had Been a Polar Explorer

I had been a polar explorer in my youth

and spent countless days and nights freezing

in one blank place and then another. Eventually,

I quit my travels and stayed at home,

and there grew within me a sudden excess of desire,

as if a brilliant stream of light of the sort one sees

within a diamond were passing through me.

I filled page after page with visions of what I had witnessed—

groaning seas of pack ice, giant glaciers, and the windswept white

of icebergs. Then, with nothing more to say, I stopped

and turned my sights on what was near. Almost at once,

a man wearing a dark coat and broad-brimmed hat

appeared under the trees in front of my house.

The way he stared straight ahead and stood,

not shifting his weight, letting his arms hang down

at his side, made me think that I knew him.

But when I raised my hand to say hello,

he took a step back, turned away, and started to fade

as longing fades until nothing is left of it.

Two Horses

On a warm night in June
I went to the lake, got on all fours,
and drank like an animal. Two horses
came up beside me to drink as well.
This is amazing, I thought, but who will believe it?
The horses eyed me from time to time, snorting
and nodding. I felt the need to respond, so I snorted, too,
but haltingly, as though not really wanting to be heard.
The horses must have sensed that I was holding back.
They moved slightly away. Then I thought they might have
    known me
in another life—the one in which I was a poet.
They might have even read my poems, for back then,
in that shadowy time when our eagerness knew no bounds,
we changed styles almost as often as there were days in the year.

I am not thinking of Death, but Death is thinking of me.

He leans back in his chair, rubs his hands, strokes

his beard, and says, "I'm thinking of Strand, I'm thinking

that one of these days I'll be out back, swinging my scythe

or holding my hourglass up to the moon, and Strand will appear

in a jacket and tie, and together under the boulevards'

leafless trees we'll stroll into the city of souls. And when

we get to the Great Piazza with its marble mansions, the crowd

that had been waiting there will welcome us with delirious cries,

and their tears, turned hard and cold as glass from having been

held back so long, will fall and clatter on the stones below.

O let it be soon. Let it be soon."

Man and Camel

On the eve of my fortieth birthday
I sat on the porch having a smoke
when out of the blue a man and a camel
happened by. Neither uttered a sound
at first, but as they drifted up the street
and out of town the two of them began to sing.
Yet what they sang is still a mystery to me—
the words were indistinct and the tune
too ornamental to recall. Into the desert
they went and as they went their voices
rose as one above the sifting sound
of windblown sand. The wonder of their singing,
its elusive blend of man and camel, seemed
an ideal image for all uncommon couples.
Was this the night that I had waited for

so long? I wanted to believe it was,

but just as they were vanishing, the man

and camel ceased to sing, and galloped

back to town. They stood before my porch,

staring up at me with beady eyes, and said:

"You ruined it. You ruined it forever."

Error

We drifted downstream under a scattering of stars
and slept until the sun rose. When we got to the capital,
which lay in ruins, we built a large fire out of what chairs
and tables we could find. The heat was so fierce that birds
overhead caught fire and fell flaming to earth.
These we ate, then continued on foot into regions
where the sea is frozen and the ground is strewn
with moonlike boulders. If only we had stopped,
turned, and gone back to the garden we started from,
with its broken urn, its pile of rotting leaves, and sat
gazing up at the house and seen only the passing
of sunlight over its windows, that would have been
enough, even if the wind cried and clouds scudded seaward
like the pages of a book on which nothing was written.

Fire

Sometimes there would be a fire and I would walk into it

and come out unharmed and continue on my way,

and for me it was just another thing to have done.

As for putting out the fire, I left that to others

who would rush into the billowing smoke with brooms

and blankets to smother the flames. When they were through

they would huddle together to talk of what they had seen—

how lucky they were to have witnessed the lusters of heat,

the hushing effect of ashes, but even more to have known the
    fragrance

of burning paper, the sound of words breathing their last.

Cake

A man leaves for the next town to pick up a cake.

On the way, he gets lost in a dense woods

and the cake is never picked up. Years later,

the man appears on a beach, staring at the sea.

"I am standing on a beach," he thinks, "and I am lost

in thought." He does not move. The heaving sea

turns black, its waves curl and crash. "Soon

I will leave," he continues. "Soon I will go

to a nearby town to pick up a cake. I will walk

in a brown and endless woods, and far away

the heaving sea will turn to black, and the waves—

I can see them now—will curl and crash."

The Rose

The sorrows of the rose were mounting up.
Twisted in a field of weeds, the helpless rose
felt the breeze of paradise just once, then died.
The children cried, "Oh rose, come back.
We love you, rose." Then someone said that soon
they'd have another rose. "Come, my darlings,
down to the pond, lean over the edge and look
at yourselves looking up. Now do you see it,
its petals open, rising to the surface, turning into you?"
"Oh no," they said. "We are what we are—nothing else."

How perfect. How ancient. How past repair.

2032

It is evening in the town of X

where Death, who used to love me, sits

in a limo with a blanket spread across his thighs,

waiting for his driver to appear. His hair

is white, his eyes have gotten small, his cheeks

have lost their luster. He has not swung his scythe

in years, or touched his hourglass. He is waiting

to be driven to the Blue Hotel, the ultimate resort,

where an endless silence fills the lilac-scented air,

and marble fish swim motionless in marble seas,

and where . . . Where is his driver? Ah, there she is,

coming down the garden steps, in heels, velvet evening gown,

and golden boa, blowing kisses to the trees.

Storm

On the last night of our house arrest
a howling wind tore through the streets,
ripping down shutters, scattering roof tiles,
leaving behind a river of refuse. When the sun
rose over the marble gate, I could see the guards,
sluggish in the morning heat, desert their posts
and stagger towards the woods just out of town.
"Darling," I said, "let's go, the guards have left,
the place is a ruin." But she was oblivious.
"You go," she said, and she pulled up the sheet
to cover her eyes. I ran downstairs and called
for my horse. "To the sea," I whispered, and off
we went and how quick we were, my horse and I,
riding over the fresh green fields, as if to our freedom.

Conversation

1

He said it would always be what might have been,
a city about to happen, a city never completed,
one that disappeared with hardly a trace, inside
or beneath the outer city, making the outer one—
the one in which we spend our waking hours—
seem pointless and dull. It would always be
a city in the dark, a city so shy that it waited,
dreading the moment that was never to be.

2

I said that the dawning of the unknown
was always before us and that the realization
of anything is a constant threat. I also said
that there is sadness in knowing that the undoing

of what has been done will never take place,

that the history of now is as distant as the future

of when. Our skills are limited, our power

to imagine enfeebled, our cities doomed.

All roads lead to the malodorous sea.

Afterwords

I

Packs of wild dogs roamed the streets of the very rich,

looking for scraps that might have been thrown their way

by a caring cook or merciful maid. Birds flew in

from everywhere, going up and down and side to side.

In the distance, beyond the stucco mansions

with their patios and pools, beyond the cemetery

with its marble angels, barely visible to the naked eye,

a man was scaling a cliff, then stopped and turned, and

opened his mouth to scream, but when the screams arrived

they were faint and cold, no different from the snow

that kept on falling through the windless night.

2

They rushed from their houses to welcome the spring,

then ran to the piers to gaze at the backs of fish,

long and glistening, then to the stables to see

the sleek, cloud-breathing horses. Nothing could keep them

from their joy, neither the storm gathering strength

in the west nor the bombs going off in the east;

theirs was the bliss of another age. Suddenly,

a woman appeared on the beach and said that soon

she would sing. "Soon she will sing," murmured

the gathering crowd. "Soon she will sing," I said

to myself as I woke. Then I went to the window

and a river of old people with canes and flashlights

were inching their way down through the dark to the sea.

3

Twenty crows sat on the limbs of an elm.

The air was so clear that one could see up

the broad valley of patchwork fields to the next town

where a train releasing a ribbon of steam

pulled out of a small wood station. Minutes later,

a man stepped onto the platform, waited, then lifted

his suitcase over his head and hurled it onto the tracks.

"That's that," he said, and turned and walked away.

The crows had taken off, it was cold, and up ahead

long, windblown shadows lashed the passive ground.

Elevator

1

The elevator went to the basement. The doors opened.

A man stepped in and asked if I was going up.

"I'm going down," I said. "I won't be going up."

2

The elevator went to the basement. The doors opened.

A man stepped in and asked if I was going up.

"I'm going down," I said. "I won't be going up."

TWO

Black Sea

One clear night while the others slept, I climbed
the stairs to the roof of the house and under a sky
strewn with stars I gazed at the sea, at the spread of it,
the rolling crests of it raked by the wind, becoming
like bits of lace tossed in the air. I stood in the long,
whispering night, waiting for something, a sign, the approach
of a distant light, and I imagined you coming closer,
the dark waves of your hair mingling with the sea,
and the dark became desire, and desire the arriving light.
The nearness, the momentary warmth of you as I stood
on that lonely height watching the slow swells of the sea
break on the shore and turn briefly into glass and disappear . . .
Why did I believe you would come out of nowhere? Why with all
that the world offers would you come only because I was here?

Mother and Son

The son enters the mother's room
and stands by the bed where the mother lies.
The son believes that she wants to tell him
what he longs to hear—that he is her boy,
always her boy. The son leans down to kiss
the mother's lips, but her lips are cold.
The burial of feelings has begun. The son
touches the mother's hands one last time,
then turns and sees the moon's full face.
An ashen light falls across the floor.
If the moon could speak, what would it say?
If the moon could speak, it would say nothing.

Mirror

A white room and a party going on
and I was standing with some friends
under a large gilt-framed mirror
that tilted slightly forward
over the fireplace.
We were drinking whiskey
and some of us, feeling no pain,
were trying to decide
what precise shade of yellow
the setting sun turned our drinks.
I closed my eyes briefly,
then looked up into the mirror:
a woman in a green dress leaned
against the far wall.
She seemed distracted,

the fingers of one hand
fidgeted with her necklace,
and she was staring into the mirror,
not at me, but past me, into a space
that might be filled by someone
yet to arrive, who at that moment
could be starting the journey
which would lead eventually to her.
Then, suddenly, my friends
said it was time to move on.
This was years ago,
and though I have forgotten
where we went and who we all were,
I still recall that moment of looking up
and seeing the woman stare past me
into a place I could only imagine,
and each time it is with a pang,
as if just then I were stepping
from the depths of the mirror

into that white room, breathless and eager,

only to discover too late

that she is not there.

Moon

Open the book of evening to the page
where the moon, always the moon, appears

between two clouds, moving so slowly that hours
will seem to have passed before you reach the next page

where the moon, now brighter, lowers a path
to lead you away from what you have known

into those places where what you had wished for happens,
its lone syllable like a sentence poised

at the edge of sense, waiting for you to say its name
once more as you lift your eyes from the page

and close the book, still feeling what it was like
to dwell in that light, that sudden paradise of sound.

People Walking Through the Night

They carried what they had in garbage bags and knapsacks,

long lines of them winding down country roads, through barren

fields to the edge of town, then onto numbered streets, by rows

of leafless trees and heaps of rubble. When they reached

the central square, they covered themselves with blankets

and pieces of cardboard, and slept on benches or leaned

on broken slabs of concrete, smoking, watching the faint

gray flags of their breath being lifted away, the swift moon

climbing the sky, their thin dogs searching for carrion.

Marsyas

Something was wrong
Screams could be heard
In the morning dark
It was cold

Screams could be heard
A storm was coming
It was cold
And the screams were piercing

A storm was coming
Someone was struggling
And the screams were piercing
Hard to imagine

Someone was struggling

So close, so close

Hard to imagine

A man was tearing open his body

So close, so close

The screams were unbearable

A man was tearing open his body

What could we do

The screams were unbearable

His flesh was in ribbons

What could we do

The rain came down

His flesh was in ribbons

And nobody spoke

The rain came down

There were flashes of lightning

And nobody spoke

Trees shook in the wind

There were flashes of lightning

Then came thunder

The Webern Variations

The sudden rush of it
pushing aside the branches,
late summer flashing towards
the image of its absence

*

Into the heart of nothing,
into the radiant hollows,
even the language of vanishing
leaves itself behind

*

Clouds, trees, houses,
in the feeling they awaken
as the dark approaches, seem
like pieces of another life

*

One can sift through what remains—
the dust of phrases uttered once,
the ruins of a passion—
it comes to less each time

                    *

The voice sliding down,
the voice turning round
and lengthening the thread
of sense, the thread of sound

                    *

Those avenues of light
that slid between the clouds
moments ago are gone,
and suddenly it is dark

                    *

Who will be left to stitch
and sew the shroud of song,
the houses back in place, the trees
rising from a purple shade?

                    *

Not too late to see oneself

walk the beach at night,

how easily the sea comes in,

spreads, retreats, and disappears

*

How easily it breathes,

and the late-risen half-moon,

drawn out of darkness, staring down,

seems to pause above the waves

*

Under the moon and stars,

which are what they have always been,

what should we be but ourselves

in this light, which is no light to speak of?

*

What should we hear but the voice

that would be ours shaping itself,

the secret voice of being telling us

that where we disappear is where we are?

*

What to make of a season's end,

the drift of cold drawn down

the hallways of the night,

the wind pushing aside the leaves?

*

The vision of one's passing passes,

days flow into other days,

the voice that sews and stitches

again picks up its work

*

And everything turns and turns

and the unknown turns into the song

that is the known, but what in turn

becomes of the song is not for us to say

My Name

Once when the lawn was a golden green
and the marbled moonlit trees rose like fresh memorials
in the scented air, and the whole countryside pulsed
with the chirr and murmur of insects, I lay in the grass,
feeling the great distances open above me, and wondered
what I would become and where I would find myself,
and though I barely existed, I felt for an instant
that the vast star-clustered sky was mine, and I heard
my name as if for the first time, heard it the way
one hears the wind or the rain, but faint and far off
as though it belonged not to me but to the silence
from which it had come and to which it would go.

THREE

Poem After the Seven Last Words

I

The story of the end, of the last word
of the end, when told, is a story that never ends.
We tell it and retell it—one word, then another
until it seems that no last word is possible,
that none would be bearable. Thus, when the hero
of the story says to himself, as to someone far away,
"Forgive them, for they know not what they do,"
we may feel that he is pleading for us, that we are
the secret life of the story and, as long as his plea
is not answered, we shall be spared. So the story
continues. So we continue. And the end, once more,
becomes the next, and the next after that.

2

There is an island in the dark, a dreamt-of place
where the muttering wind shifts over the white lawns
and riffles the leaves of trees, the high trees
that are streaked with gold and line the walkways there;
and those already arrived are happy to be the silken
remains of something they were but cannot recall;
they move to the sound of stars, which is also imagined,
but who cares about that; the polished columns they see
may be no more than shafts of sunlight, but for those
who live on and on in the radiance of their remains
this is of little importance. There is an island
in the dark and you will be there, I promise you, you
shall be with me in paradise, in the single season of being,
in the place of forever, you shall find yourself. And there
the leaves will turn and never fall, there the wind
will sing and be your voice as if for the first time.

3

Someday someone will write a story telling
among other things of a parting between mother
and son, of how she wandered off, of how he vanished
in air. But before that happens, it will describe
how their faces shone with a feeble light and how
the son was moved to say, "Woman, look at your son,"
then to a friend nearby, "Son, look at your mother."
At which point the writer will put down his pen
and imagine that while those words were spoken
something else happened, something unusual like
a purpose revealed, a secret exchanged, a truth
to which they, the mother and son, would be bound,
but what it was no one would know. Not even the writer.

4

These are the days of spring when the sky is filled
with the odor of lilac, when darkness becomes desire,
and there is nothing that does not wish to be born;
days when the fate of the present is a breezy fullness,
when the world's great gift for fiction gilds even
the dirt we walk on, and we feel we could live forever
while knowing of course that we can't. Such is our plight.
The master of weather and everything else, if he wants,
can bring forth a dark of a different kind, one hidden
by darkness so deep it cannot be seen. No one escapes.
Not even the man who believed he was chosen to do so,
for when the dark came down he cried out, "Father, Father,
why have you forsaken me?" To which no answer came.

5

To be thirsty. To say, "I thirst."

To close one's eyes and see the giant world

that is born each time the eyes are closed.

To see one's death. To see the darkening clouds

as the tragic cloth of a day of mourning. To be the one

mourned. To open the dictionary of the Beyond and discover

what one suspected, that the only word in it

is nothing. To try to open one's eyes, but not to be

able to. To feel the mouth burn. To feel the sudden

presence of what, again and again, was not said.

To translate it and have it remain unsaid. To know

at last that nothing is more real than nothing.

6

"It is finished," he said. You could hear him say it,

the words almost a whisper, then not even that,

but an echo so faint it seemed no longer to come

from him, but from elsewhere. This was his moment,

his final moment. "It is finished," he said into a vastness

that led to an even greater vastness, and yet all of it

within him. He contained it all. That was the miracle,

to be both large and small in the same instant, to be

like us, but more so, then finally to give up the ghost,

which is what happened. And from the storm that swirled

in his wake a formal nakedness took shape, the truth

of disguise and the mask of belief were joined forever.

7

Back down these stairs to the same scene,

to the moon, the stars, the night wind. Hours pass

and only the harp off in the distance and the wind

moving through it. And soon the sun's gray disk,

darkened by clouds, sailing above. And beyond,

as always, the sea of endless transparence, of utmost

calm, a place of constant beginning that has within it

what no eye has seen, what no ear has heard, what no hand

has touched, what has not arisen in the human heart.

To that place, to the keeper of that place, I commit myself.

Notes

"The Webern Variations," commissioned by the Brentano String Quartet, was performed in Alice Tully Hall, Lincoln Center, in February 2005. One quatrain was read between each movement of the three Webern quartets.

"Poem After the Seven Last Words," also commissioned by the Brentano String Quartet, was performed at the University of Michigan, the University of Chicago, Princeton University, and the Rothko Chapel in Houston, Texas, in 2003–04. One section was read between each movement of Haydn's quartet op. 51, called "The Seven Last Words of Christ." The poem relies heavily on the Gnostic Gospel of Thomas.

"Error" is dedicated to Bill and Sandy Bailey.

"The Webern Variations" is dedicated to Tricia Dailey.

"Man and Camel" is dedicated to Varujan Boghosian.

A Note About the Author

*Mark Strand was born in Summerside, Prince Edward Island,
Canada, and was raised and educated in the United States.
He is the author of ten earlier books of poems. He is also the
author of a book of stories,* Mr. and Mrs. Baby, *three volumes
of translations (of works by Rafael Alberti and Carlos Drummond
de Andrade, and of anonymous Quechua lyrics), a number of anthologies
(most recently* 100 Great Poems of the Twentieth Century*), and
monographs on the contemporary artists William Bailey and Edward
Hopper. He has received many honors and grants for his poems,
including a MacArthur Fellowship for 1987–92, and in 1990 he
was chosen Poet Laureate of the United States. In 1993 he was
awarded the Bollingen Prize, and in 1999 he won the Pulitzer
Prize for* Blizzard of One. *He lives in New York City
and teaches at Columbia University.*

A Note on the Type

This book was set in Janson, a typeface long thought to have been made by the Dutchman Anton Janson, who was a practicing typefounder in Leipzig during the years 1668–87. However, it has been conclusively demonstrated that these types are actually the work of Nicholas Kis (1650–1702), a Hungarian, who most probably learned his trade from the master Dutch typefounder Dirk Voskens. The type is an excellent example of the influential and sturdy Dutch types that prevailed in England up to the time William Caslon (1692–1766) developed his own incomparable designs from them.

Composed by Creative Graphics, Allentown, Pennsylvania
Printed and bound by United Book Press, Baltimore, Maryland
Designed by Anthea Lingeman